A Minister Wife

MARRIED LONELY BUT NOT ALONE

Patricia Stocker

A MINISTER WIFE
MARRIED LONELY BUT NOT ALONE

Scripture taken from the New King James Version. Copyright © 1979, 1980, 1982 by Thomas Nelson, Inc. Used by permission. All rights reserved.

Scripture taken from the King James Version of the Bible.

Scripture taken from the Holy Bible, NEW INTERNATIONAL VERSION®. Copyright © 1973, 1978, 1984, 2011 by Biblica, Inc. All rights reserved worldwide. Used by permission. NEW INTERNATIONAL VERSION® and NIV® are registered trademarks of Biblica, Inc. Use of either trademark for the offering of goods or services requires the prior written consent of Biblica US, Inc.

iUniverse books may be ordered through booksellers or by contacting:

iUniverse
1663 Liberty Drive
Bloomington, IN 47403
www.iuniverse.com
1-800-Authors (1-800-288-4677)

Because of the dynamic nature of the Internet, any web addresses or links contained in this book may have changed since publication and may no longer be valid. The views expressed in this work are solely those of the author and do not necessarily reflect the views of the publisher, and the publisher hereby disclaims any responsibility for them.

Any people depicted in stock imagery provided by Getty Images are models, and such images are being used for illustrative purposes only. Certain stock imagery © Getty Images.

ISBN: 978-1-5320-4674-2 (sc)
ISBN: 978-1-5320-4675-9 (-e)

Library of Congress Control Number: 2018904074

Print information available on the last page.

iUniverse rev. date: 04/02/2018

Introduction

Do you find yourself unable to handle the dilemma that you are facing now in your marriage? Are you clueless about how you can change the atmosphere in your home? Do you need help overcoming the trials and tests in your marriage? Will you allow God to fix you during the process of making you a virtuous wife?

There are benefits when you learn how to submit to your husband as if you are submitting to the Lord. When you submit or humble yourself, the Lord will move on your behalf and calm the storm in your marriage. You can discover ways in the Word of God that will help you be victorious and the virtuous wife God created you to be.

I wrote this book because I believe that there are women out there who might be dealing with the same things or some similar experiences of being a minister's or pastor's wife. I did not want to tell anyone about what was going on in my home or marriage, so I suffered silently and alone. At times, I wanted to throw in the towel.

I thought about taking my own life because of what seemed like the most unbearable life imaginable. But as I began to pray and apply God's Word, I saw the change. But the change did not immediately alter my situation or my husband. The change began in me.

When I got married, I was so happy. Who would've thought I would marry a man of the cloth? I had come out of abusive relationships, hopping from man to man, seeking love in all the wrong places. I did not realize that God had a divine plan for my life to become a minister's wife and now a pastor's wife. Through the storms, tests, and trials I faced, God helped me realize that what I went through was not only for me but others as well. I can share now how I overcame loneliness, feelings of rejection, and the infidelity. With God's grace and mercy, I was able to forgive and love that which hurt me and caused so much pain.

At times during this devastating process, I felt as if I were having a mental breakdown. In an effort to forgive and let go of the things that had devastated me, the internal conflict of spirit and flesh often created overwhelming periods of uncontrollable sobbing and depression. At the same time, I had to pray and pray and pray just to be able to be in the same house, let alone the same bed. Moreover I had to apply the Word of God to my situation. I then began to experience the manifestation of God moving in me.

For the most part, I can tell you that there is healing in this book for you. I urge you to keep reading and see how God turned one mess into one flesh through His Word of instruction. He is not a God that will do it for one and not for you.

In conclusion, when you let go of what is in your hand, God will let go of what is in his hand, and your life will never be the same in Jesus's name. I am reminded of a scripture in the Bible that says, "Weeping endures only for a night, but joy comes in the morning (Ps. 30:5)."

Married

To unite, take, or give in wedlock; to enter into matrimony

Therefore a man shall leave his father and mother and be joined to his wife and they shall become one flesh.
—Genesis 3:24

The Beginning

First, I know that all marriages are different. Some are more preferable than others are. When I was asked for my hand in marriage, I was beyond excited. My dream had come true. I began to plan for the most important day of my life, becoming someone's wife. I wondered in my mind how many flower girls, ring bearers, and bridesmaids I would have and where we would we go on the honeymoon. I thought about everything that pertained to that day. The excitement and joy in my heart I felt was indescribable. I began to think about all the things a wife was supposed to do: cook his food, make sure the house was clean, and do the laundry, everything that would make my new husband happy.

As a child, I would watch my mom cook for my dad and the church on Sunday afternoon after the service. I said to myself, "I want to be married and have two children."

My mother, a stay-at-home mom, made it look so easy and fun to me. Her job was her children, along with clean the house, cook, wash dishes, and, of course, take care of my dad. I never heard her complain about her duty as a wife during my childhood. As a result of watching her, I wanted to be someone's wife as well.

On August 5, 1996, in the middle of the afternoon, my pastor and his wife, one of the sisters and brothers of the church, my husband-to-be, a construction worker, and myself witnessed my marriage. Unfortunately the wedding I planned didn't happen. We decided to plan for a big celebration later. I stood there in a stupor. I was about to be married. My dad and mom were working, and his family lived in Compton, California. We said our vows and "I do."

I said to myself, "I am marring a preacher!"

To my surprise, I didn't realize there would be so many trials in a godly marriage. It never entered into my mind that I would experience being an unhappy wife. I had married a preacher. I knew he knew how to treat his wife. This was what I expected from him being a man of God. I had to remember they are human too. They are not perfect!

At this time, I was a baby in Christ, meaning God was redirecting my life from partying, broken relationships, and just doing me. I was on the road of becoming a new creation according to 2 Corinthians 5:17 (KJV), "Therefore, if anyone is in Christ, he is a new creation. The old has passed away; behold, all things are become new." I had been in abusive and broken relationships that triggered thoughts of this marriage not lasting long because of the past relationships that didn't.

I called the first two or three months the honeymoon stage. During that period, we spent all day texting and writing each other love letters. I packed his lunches with sexy notes in the bag, and we would pillow talk throughout the night. Sounds good, huh, ladies?

The next four or five months were heavenly. We would go on weekend getaways and dinner dates. We'd hold hands and constantly say, "I love you" back and forth with one another. Sadly all hell broke loose in the sixth month, and he started showing signs that he regretted being married. For example, he would not show any emotions, and if I would come in his presence, he would be irritable. He would treat me as if I were his enemy. He slept on the couch instead of next to me in bed. The pillow talk stopped, along with the constant sweet messages. We were no longer in the honeymoon phase of this godly marriage.

As time went on, things were very unstable. His conversations with me were short and sharp, but he would talk nicer to his coworkers, a stranger, or the people in church rather than his own wife. I recalled the times he looked at me with love and admiration in his eyes. Now his look said, "Get out my face." What should I do? How should I handle it? Everything between us had changed, even my outlook on a godly marriage.

When my marriage started changing, I started to think, *is it me? Why is he treating me this way?* I was so disappointed and upset how his conduct had turned toward me. For instance, the summers are very hot here. My husband would work all day in it so I would half-freeze his favorite drink for him. When he came home, I would stand at the backdoor with the drink in my hand for him. When he entered the door with a smile on my face and drink in my hand, he looked at me and said, "Sit it over there." And he'd walk back outside.

At that very moment, I was hurt and upset because of his response. I was expecting to hear "Thank you, baby," get a kiss on the cheek, or something. It never happened! Over time, due to his constant disrespectful and dishonoring behavior, it brought me to a place of hurt. Are you ladies or men ready for this? It was Valentine's Day of 1999. Our youngest daughter was two years old. I had paid for a babysitter to watch her for me, and the sitter lived right around the corner. I made my famous pot of seafood gumbo and a pot of white rice, and I was the dessert.

I had confetti on the table, red and white balloons were everywhere, and his favorite glass, Simply Lemonade, was ready. I made sure his drink was half frozen, just the way he liked it. Ladies, I waited four hours for him to come home. Can you believe this high yellow man walked right past me with no emotion expressed? He didn't say "Thank you, baby" or even show an ounce of gratitude. Instead he walked right past me and went straight to the bathroom, where he took a shower.

I was extremely disappointed beyond measure and hurt again because my husband did not seem to care. Can you imagine the pain of going all out of the way for someone you love and not get the same in return or at least feel appreciated? Now, once you have been hurt over and over and you haven't asked God to heal you, the next phase is anger. Once you allow anger to come in, you welcome his brother and sisters or sometimes cousins inside your heart—bitterness, hatred, unforgiveness, aggravation, frustration, irritation, and murder.

Now I didn't reach murder stage, but honey, I felt like I was almost there. I prayed one day out of ignorance, "Lord, how can I kill him and get away with it?"

I am so glad the Lord is a righteous judge. This is how the book started inside of me. I began to study the Word of God concerning our marriage and what we were doing wrong in our marriage. Now Ephesians 5:25 say, "Husbands, love your wives, just as Christ also loved the church and gave Himself for her."

Jesus laid down his life for us so we could live. Husbands are supposed to lay down their lives so their wives can live. This means they should love their wives before themselves, protecting her, making sure she is okay, remaining sensitive to her needs, understanding her, and, most importantly, listening to her. When he shows her the love and affection he has in his heart concerning her needs, it is much easier for her to submit to her husband as the Word of God has said. But we should submit anyway even if he doesn't love us the way the Bible said.

However, if a man fails to humble himself, it allows room for the enemy to come in and cause division in the home. As a matter of fact, division starts in the heart of a man or female by saying something like this, "I will never let anybody hurt me like my kids' mother or father." By keeping this in our heart, there will be a separation in the marriage due to fear of being hurt again, and loneliness creeps in during the separation period.

This reminds me of a just-in-case situation. For instance, when things get heated and you both say things from your heart like "I'm glad I didn't let her in my heart," this is a just in case! (Reservation is the action of reserving something.) When loneliness is received, it allows the enemy to twist things around, and it can even make you do a thing that is out of character and displeases God.

For example, during the time I was hurting and feeling lonely, these thoughts came to mind: "Find you a friend to talk to. It won't hurt anything. Lie." He will inject these thoughts in your mind to make you feel alone and lonely, as if your husband does not care about you. Remember how subtle the enemy was through the serpent in Genesis 3:1–3? I often wondered, *where was Adam while the serpent spoke with Eve?*

Well, guess what? The revelation God spoke to me concerning this situation was divine. When the serpent spoke to Eve, it simply meant the enemy injected a thought into her mind to think she would not surely die if she ate the fruit, but she would be as God, knowing good and evil. Like Adam, some husbands are wrapped up in their own thing and mentally and emotionally neglecting their wives. On the other hand, you don't feel close, connected, or secure. You realize you are apart on basic understandings. He doesn't pay attention to you. His compliments are few and far between. You don't know how to communicate about what's hurting you and how you are feeling.

At times, my husband would walk his bright-red self in the house. Some days he might speak; other days he might not. I would get in my flesh and say something that was not pleasing to the Lord or my husband. Afterward, I would think to myself, *why did I say that?*

I look back on it and realized it caused a bigger mess—arguing, walking past one another, making sure we didn't touch one another as we passed each other, or not speaking for days or even weeks. We were so close to the edge of the bed that, if one rolled over, I would be on the floor. It was just a mess!

With this in mind, I know two things will quickly break down a marriage: refusing sex and not communicating. Yes! These two things can open a door for adultery. Yes, ladies, I said the big A word, adultery! We are so entangled in our emotions to where we refuse to acknowledge them and avoid giving our husband intimacy because he has hurt you.

The lack of communication allows one or both spouses to look for communication elsewhere. You ladies aren't hearing me though! The enemy will make sure someone he knows is his type. He will go out of his way to speak to you! For instance, your husband or wife won't compliment how you look. Instead you might go to work and hear it from someone else. Your coworker can tell you that you smell good or he even likes the way you changed your hair. The enemy will make someone else notice everything about you that your spouse has failed to mention.

Ephesians 5:28–29 says, "So husbands ought to love their own wives as their own bodies; he who loves his wife loves himself. For no one ever hated his own flesh, but nourishes and cherishes it, just as the Lord does the church."

I read this and began to think, *did my husband read this part of the Word? Or did he not want to deal with it in his heart concerning this scripture?* It could be many reasons why he failed to do this part of the scripture. I wonder if he lost the fear of God. I do not know. Maybe he wasn't ready for God to deal with this part in his heart. I became rebellious toward my husband after a period of time. He would quote scriptures in the middle of me telling him about himself.

He'd say, "Don't worry about what I do. Worry about yourself."

I said, "You hypocrite! You have the audacity to tell me that. Do you have any conviction preaching or teaching when you are in error concerning how you mistreat me?"

Luke 6:28 say to pray for those who mistreat you. I didn't want to pray with him or for him. I saw a man with two faces, one of an angel and the other of an evil beast. On the other hand, there was how he treated me versus other women on his job and in the church. My husband would tell other women what he saw nice about them, asked how they were doing, and even noticed their hair and nails. But he would not compliment me. I was upset about it.

I talked to him concerning this matter. The one thing I did not do first was pray nor have a calm spirit.

He said, "You just jealous."

You all know my emotion went to third gear. I stood there and thought to myself, *I want to do something bad to this man.* So I left the room feeling rejected. I went in my secret place and prayed, "God, please help me. I'm hurting and feeling thrown away."

The enemy loves to attack your mind with words to destroy your faith. Daniel 7:25 says, "He shall speak words against the Most High and shall were out the saints of the most High."

Words are powerful. God spoke the world into existence according to Genesis 1:3. And God said, "Let there be light." He spoke, and it was done. Proverbs 18:21 says, "Death and life are in the power of the tongue, and those who love it shall eat the fruits." In other words, by speaking well or evil comes the fruit of it, either good or bad. Be careful how you speak to one another!

Love Suffer Long

"Charity suffereth long, and is kind; charity envieth not; charity vaunteth not itself, is not puffed up."

In 1 Corinthians 13:4 (KJV), charity (love) suffereth long and is kind. When I read the words "suffereth long," I ask the question: how long is long? And what do you mean, "suffer long?" It means patiently enduring a lasting offense or hardship. It refers to a great deal of patience or endurance of something or someone. I thought to myself, *I couldn't do that! How can I love someone who doesn't love me back? Why do I have to be kind to him when he's acting unkind?* I asked these actual questions!

A still voice said, "Read the beatitude."

I replied, "Huh, beatitude?"

So I read Matthew 5:11, "Bless are you when men revile you." When he speaks abusively toward you, you speak kindness because it is like heaping burning coal on his head, according to Proverbs 25:22. For instance, when my husband would speak unkindly toward me, my response would be with love, which caused him to feel shameful and have a repentant heart. Mind you, I sometime gave back what was giving out, which did not turn out good for me. I had to go and ask him to forgive me, and I asked God to forgive me for my behavior and response. You know, it brought to mind that Jesus did not ask how long he would have to suffer, and he did it until his death on the cross. Jesus was beaten, whipped, and abused, all for love he had for you and me. That's love, the agape love, that unconditional love he showed on his way to Calvary.

As I continued to read, it said, "Love is kind. It does not envy. It does not boast. It is not proud." Reading this passage triggered me to do an evaluation deep inside of my heart. Did I suffer long? Had I endured or showed patience during the times of trouble or trials in my marriage? No, I did not pass the test of being patient, kind, or honoring my husband. I flunked the test over and over and over again. Until I passed the test, I had to retake it. Due to past dysfunctional relationships that should've had no part in my life and without complete healing, the hurt from my past was still there, buried deep in my heart.

When something similar happened, it would trigger that hurt in my mind I thought was no longer there. Therefore, in order to walk in unconditional love, I had to be totally healed from past hurts. Past hurt and present hurt are the same hurts. It feels the same, acts the same, and behaves the same. The Bible said, "But when that which is perfect comes, then that which is imperfect shall pass away (1 Cor. 13:10)."

Endure: to remain firm under; to bear with patience; to put up with; to sustain; to suffer; to tolerate; to continue; to last

The word "endureth" stood out to me, to remain firm under pressure and to have patience while putting up with my husband while God was working on me. He sustained me to be able to tolerate him while we continued on this journey called marriage.

Yes, it is a challenge, but I know I can do all things through Christ who strengthen me. The nights I laid in the bed by myself while the baby was sleeping on the coach or the floor, I was wondering what was going on. I started to pray on it, continually asking God for understanding because it was affecting me mentally. I wanted to go and ask my husband what was up, but my attitude would've been terrible. So I stayed in the room and talked to the Lord about it.

Jesus stepped in and gave me peace. I went to sleep peacefully. It's amazing to me how you can be married and feel alone, but you are not alone. I was wondering how this could happen. You see, God has joined two imperfect people with two different characteristics, upbringings, and environments.

Coming together as one is a challenge all within itself. Proverbs 27:17 (KJV) says, "As iron sharpen iron, so one person sharpens another." For instance, there are benefits in rubbing two pieces of metal together. Ecclesiastes 4:9 say, "Two are better than one, because they have a good reward for their toil." We should simply relate with one another and be good to each other. We must forgive each other, restore each other, submit to one another, encourage each other, admonish and exhort each other, and stir one another on to love and good deeds. Therefore we should pursue the things that make for peace and things that edify one another, according to Romans 14:19.

Bless the Peacemaker

Blessed are the peacemakers, for they shall be called sons of God.
—Matthew 5:9 (Spirit-Filled Life Bible)

Peacemakers are those who show a peaceable temper. They are quick to make peace and live peaceably with all men. They strive to prevent contention, strife, and war. No matter what happened or who or what caused the contention or quarrel, I had the opportunity of reconciling the matter with my husband. I didn't want to be a peacemaker. I chose to bring war, arguments, strife, and hostility. With no freedom in my mind, I was distracted with the ongoing strife and fighting no tranquility from within. Without peace, I was subject to lose my mind, worrying about the problems in my marriage and not trusting God with it. God wanted me to turn to him and cast all my cares on him.

Philippians 4:6 say, "Do not be anxious about anything." This means to not be troubled with cares. God would not allow opposition to come into my marriage if he thought I weren't able to handle it. The Lord was there all the time, but I did not know it. I was caught up in my emotions and how hurt I was. I was thinking about myself, having self-pity parties and not realizing he was there all the time. God wanted me to have true peace by praying about everything. He was concerned about me, including the big and the small, where to move, what to say, and what to do. This was peace like no other, a peace that surpasses all understanding and going beyond what was expected.

My enemy thought infidelity would take me out, but according to John 14:27, "Peace I leave with you, my peace I give you. I do not give to you as the world gives, because the world can't give you peace. Do not let your heart (mind, will, emotion) be troubled and do not be afraid." And Deuteronomy 31:6 reads, "The Lord will never leave you nor forsake you."

"'Oh house of Israel, can I not do with you as this potter?' says the Lord. 'Look, as the clay is in the potter's hand, so are you in my hand'" (Jer. 18:6 Spirit-Filled Life Bible).

I began to cry to the Lord, acknowledging where I was wrong and began to ask him to forgive me. God will not forgive us when we do not forgive someone who wronged us. I had to let go of what had happened in the past. Yes, I was hurt and mistreated, but it was over. It happened. Now I had to let it go. I used pain and hurt as a blanket of justification for my bad behaviors. When I heard "Get over it!" I was shocked!

"Get over it," I replied.

He said, "Just how long you took to hurt is the length of time it will take for you to help with healing that caused you to continue to behave in an ungodly behavior."

Just to hear that was so devastating to me. I could not understand how he could say those words to me. I learned if my husband had taken the time to help me heal and build up that trust level, our marriage would have been in a much better state.

Nevertheless, it was so true that I had to get over it. Over a period of time, God told me the same exact thing. I had stopped the process of becoming a beautiful diamond. God saw more than I could see in me. He saw a diamond in the rough.

A diamond is one of the most expensive and precious gems. It starts out as a piece of coal deep in the earth. A bit of extreme pressure and time compresses and makes a diamond. The diamond is the toughest of gems because of the extreme pressure and heat that causes the diamond molecules to change.

Through the fire of affliction and the furnace, he began to refine me in my secret place. With my insecurities, bad mind-set, and old habits, he began to take away from my true design. This was my season of affliction. I prayed, "Lord, make me better and not bitter. Make me the way you want me to be,"

He heard the prayer. When I said "make me better," the surgery started. With the cutting away, he took off things that were not like him. It was very painful but necessary in order for me to grow and shine.

Stay in the Refining Furnace

See, I have refined you, though not as silver; I
have tested you in the furnace of affliction.
—Isaiah 48:10 NIV

Refining: remove impurities or unwanted elements; improve

During the time of opposition, my marriage was upside down, along with the problems on my job and the issues with the church. No matter how the storm rages and the wind may blow, do not jump ship! In other words, do not be in a hurry to leave quickly before facing or dealing with the adversity. There will be trouble, trials, and some difficulties in marriages. I never heard of nor saw a faultless marriage, although I have come across a few that had portrayed their marriage to be picture-perfect. But in reality, they were facing hard times, trials, troubles, and tribulation.

To explain, as a minister, I had to attend certain classes in order to minister. One was a marriage class. Remember—my marriage wasn't in good shape, and some knew that. During the class, I had a check in my spirit. The couple that taught the class made me feel terrible because my marriage wasn't honorable enough to be in ministry according to them. I sat there, listened, and prayed within, "Lord, if you ever place me in a position to minister to people in broken marriages, I would never make them feel how I feel now, terrible."

With this in mind, sometime later the couple that taught the class ended up divorcing. I never thought that would've happened to them because I always saw the love they portrayed. Never judge a marriage according to how it is portrayed because you do not know the real picture behind the frame.

Isaiah 48:10 say, "I have refined thee." Refining does not come from listening to your pastor or reading the Bible. Refining comes from being exposed to strenuous situations and enduring pain and suffering. My marriage was God's way of refining me. He used certain situations to remove debris out of my life he had no use of—the garbage that had been left from past relationships, the pain from childhood, and feelings of rejection and abandonment. I didn't know that all this was lying dormant inside of my heart until I accepted Christ as my Lord and Savior.

Have you heard the phrases, "Ugly has to come out in order for the good to get in" or "What's in you has to come out"? Well, I have! All the things I had heard and learned from my daddy and bad relationships, God had to burn off all the debris and useless parts he couldn't use.

For instance, as a child, I was taught to be respectful. I was not to steal and do well in school. I was to stay in a child place and go to church. Growing up, I saw things I should've seen, and I heard things that I should've heard. My dad told my sisters and me, "Never let a man make a fool out of you." He said, "Baby, a man can work twenty-four hours a day and still have time for another woman." The kicker was, "Don't depend on a man for nothing. Work and get your own stuff."

Before I accepted Christ, I made sure I remembered what my daddy said because he knew what he was talking about. That's my daddy, and he's a man. He knows. Through the years moving from one broken relationship to another, having a baby and not a husband, and being physically abused has caused a numerous amount of pain in my heart. Rather you believe me or not, I carried these things in my heart for many years. I never knew I had to be healed from the past hurts and disappointments.

When I received Christ in my heart and accepted the Holy Spirit to govern me, I asked him to cleanse me and wash me white as snow according to Psalm 51, and the Lord answered my prayer. The process of refining had begun. He said, "See, I have refined you, though not as silver."

"Though not as silver." I asked myself what that meant. Lord, help me too understand what you are saying. Only the spirit of God can give revelation and clarification to his Word. The Spirit revealed to me that the silver furnace is the best way for removing rubbish, but it's not favorite enough for the Lord with his people. His refining is with utmost care and separating power. The Lord uses the furnace to prepare the soul (heart) to make it tender and ready to change. It is the furnace of affliction, hardships, trouble, adversity, distress, and trials.

I had to go through a season of refining for a transformation and purification although it was uncomfortable for the time being, but God was more concerned about my condition than my comfort. I had to be more patient in the furnace and allow God to purify my heart (soul-mind, will, and emotion).

Purifying the Heart

Create in me a clean heart, O God, and
renew a steadfast spirit within me.
—Psalm 51:10

Original Word: καρδία, ας, ἡ
Part of Speech: Noun, Feminine
Transliteration: kardia
Phonetic Spelling: (kar-dee'-ah)
Short Definition: the heart, inner life, intention
Definition: lit; the heart; mind; character; inner self; will; intention; center (Strong's Concordance)

What I'm about to share concerning the heart I have never heard nor taught until my husband came into my life. David had asked for a clean heart. He alluded to an inward newness. David wanted a pure heart. The Bible says only the pure in heart shall see God. He wants his affections and feelings made right. Geneses 1:26 (NIV) says, "Then God said, 'Let us make mankind in our image, in our likes, so that they may rule over all the creatures that move along the ground.'"

God created man by fashioning a body out of mud and clay, transforming the clay into something new and then breathing his (spirit) life in to it. Genesis 2:7 say, "And the Lord God formed man of the dust of the ground, and breathed into his nostril the breath of life and the man become a living soul." Man, as created by God, is a triune being prepared "spirit, soul, and body." First Thessalonians 5:23 says, "May the God of peace himself sanctify you completely; and may your whole spirit, soul and body be preserved blameless at the coming of our Lord Jesus Christ."

Now we know that we are three parts (the whole man): spirit, soul, and body. Just say, "I am a spirit. I possess a soul and live in a body." I pray I have not lost anyone yet. We need to know how we function and our makeup.

The Whole Man

The outer circle is the body: touch, taste, hearing, seeing, and smelling (the five senses). The middle circle is where your soul dwells: mind, will, and emotion. The inner circle is your spirit: intuition, conscience, communication, and many other attributes (Gal. 5:22).

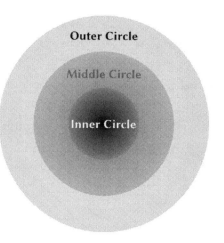

The body is world-conscious; the soul is self-conscious. And the spirit is God-conscious. Each one has elements. The body has five elements—taste, touch, seeing, smelling, and hearing—which sums up the flesh. The soul has three elements—mind, will, and emotion—which sums up understanding. The spirit has four—conscience, intuition, communication, and many other attributes—according to Galatians 5:22 (fruit of the Spirit), which sums up overseer.

We are spiritual beings and should not be identified by what we are, but by who we are. And that determines what comes out the heart. The Bible says, "For out of the abundance of the heart, his mouth speaks" (Luke 6:45). In other words, the things we harbor in our heart will come out during a time of adversity, trials, and testing. The soul is the inner life of a human being. It is the seat of emotions and the center of human personality and the hidden man of the heart, according to 1 Peter 3:4.

The soul has to be trained because it does not accept the things of the spirit of God. It is the master of the body. And not to mention, the soul is self-conscious wrapped up in emotions—our feelings, central perception, and passions. Our mind has to be renewed and transformed. Ephesians 4:23 says to be made new in the attitude of your minds. Renewing the mind is changing the old way of thinking and having the mind of Christ. Isaiah 55:8 say that God's thoughts are not as man, though man is made in God's image, but the character in every way boundlessly exceeds that of man.

Mind

1. Thoughts
2. Logic
3. Imagination
4. Intellect
5. Logic (which sums up understanding)

Therefore, get wisdom, and with all thy getting, get understanding. Renewing the mind takes faith, and faith is doing the Word of God. By applying his Word, it will help change the way you think concerning your life, your job, and the relationship with your children and husband. His Word will cause a change from the inside out. The more you fill up your mind with the Word of God by reading, meditating, memorizing, and praying, the more your thinking will start to change. With a renewed mind comes a godly perspective about your job, your marriage, your children, your money, and other areas in your life. It will give you a new attitude and a clearer outlook on everything.

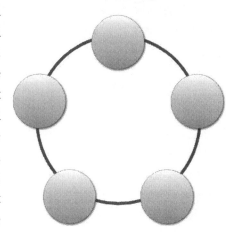

And do not be conformed to this world (world-conscious), but be transformed by the renewing of your mind that you may prove what is good and acceptable and what is the perfect will of God according to Romans 12:12.

The way you think determines the way you feel because feelings do not produce thoughts, but thoughts produce feelings. Whatever you thought about that caused your emotions to be aroused, those feelings just don't come from out of nowhere. Your feelings do not produce the thoughts but the thoughts produces the feelings. You can think yourself either happy or mad as a matter of fact.

Think about a situation that had a hurtful effect on you. I guarantee it will trigger a thought of the past and cause your emotion to react as if it just happened. By explaining what goes on in the mind, this will help you understand why certain things happen in our thought life. If we do not renew our thinking or change the way you think, we will undoubtedly experience many different battles.

The battle of what is right versus what is wrong is spiritual warfare taking place in your thoughts. The Bible tells us to pull down strongholds, cast down imaginations and every high thing that exalts itself against the knowledge of God, and bring into captivity every thought to the obedience of Christ. A stronghold is an incorrect thinking pattern (lie) that has formed itself into our way of thinking.

Now we know a stronghold is based upon a lie. Through the Word of God, we will tear down such faulty thinking patterns. Through the washing of the Word, our minds are renewed and transformed, and strongholds (lies) are torn down. Ephesians 5:26 says, "That he might sanctify and cleanse it with the washing of water by the word." Meditating and washing our minds with the Word of God will cause a transformation in our thought life, and we will know God's will for our marriage and discern what is right, perfect, and good. The adversary will always try to inject negative thoughts that are not of God toward our husband to keep us in bondage and contention. Daily we must put on the armor of God. The helmet of salvation will protect your mind because we are in a spiritual warfare.

Spiritual Warfare

For we wrestle not against flesh and
blood, but against principalities
—Ephesians 6:12

Our fight or battles are not with our husband, family, or friends; they are with an unseen demonic force from Satan and his kingdom. Satan works through an army of demonic spirits. He cannot be everywhere at the same time. He is not omnipresent. Only God is. He is the accuser of the brethren (children of God), not the children of the world, according to Revelation 12:10.

By using the whole armor of God, we can beat Satan and his army. Ephesians 6:10 talks about weapons. We can use the helmet of salvation to tear down strongholds formed in our mind from accepting the lies and deception from the enemy. He hates marriages because God has ordained marriages. You can find the design for marriage in Genesis 2:18–25. This chapter will help us learn how to honor, build a marriage of love, and have everlasting joy if we apply God's principles.

The helmet is vital during spiritual warfare. It protects and covers the head from all the fiery darts the enemy tries to throw. If the head is badly injured, the rest of the body will not be of use.

The helmet and the sword of the spirit, which is the Word of God, work together. The helmet of salvation protects your mind and thinking. The sword of the spirit fortifies your thinking. Whenever your prayer life and praying together stops the enemy gets in and causes such uproar. You feel hopeless and insignificant to pray. Satan then injects fiery darts in your thoughts that are not the thoughts of God, asking, "Why pray about it when you can get even?"

Your prayer life helps build up your confidence. It gives you courage and a firm foundation of faith. Praying together causes a threefold cord not easily broken, meaning double and triple power! The Bible said one can put a thousand a flight and two can put ten thousand a flight in agreeing. Prayer makes it hard for the enemy to start strife and nitpicking and cause division between husband and wife. The Bible said, if you bite and devour each other, watch out, or you will be destroyed by each other.

The warfare in my marriage was designed to kill me. The Bible said the thief comes to steal, kill, and destroy. He tries to steal my joy because he knows that's where my strength is. He tries to kill my peace by shooting lies in my mind. Then he will try to destroy what God has joined together.

I didn't always keep my helmet on tight some days. I might just slightly put it on, not making sure it was tight. That was the day the enemy knocked it right off. I had gone to battle with flesh, another human, my husband. The arguing and the name-calling back and forth lasted too long. My peace was disturbed, and my joy turned into sadness. I battled in my mind all night with myself, saying, "Leave his butt. He's not used to a good woman." For other negative things that came up, I agreed with.

My spirit was saying, "Pray, believe God, and stand on the Word of God, and he will war for you."

After a week or so, I prayed, but by that time, I was so emotionally drained and physically tired because of the strife, bickering, and fighting in the flesh. Prayer and the Word of God helped me to regain my joy and peace in the midst of a battle in my marriage. If I desire to have a marriage in unity with the same spirit and thinking, we have to submit one to another, as the Word said to do. Not just for me, but for him as well. Now remember that even when he is not surrendering or submitting, I had to. In spite of what it looks like, do the Word, and you will not go wrong. The flesh always wants to win the war, but the spirit wins the battle.

"Walk in the Spirit and you will not fulfill the lust of the flesh" (Gal. 5:16 KJV).

I didn't understand what that verse meant. "Walk in the spirit." Nobody could walk in the spirit all the time. Well, I gathered I could according to Galatians 5:22. If I walk in love, joy, peace, gentleness, goodness, faith, long-suffering, meekness, and temperance as much as I can. For the most part, my human nature is subject to the lust of the flesh; therefore, when my flesh presents itself, I hear the words, "I am only human."

The works of the flesh are adultery, fornication, hatred, strife, murders, envy, and more. I realize that the two always war against one another the spirit and the flesh. I will walk in the spirit of love and not my flesh according to the things of the world. I didn't want my flesh to destroy my marriage, although I had been betrayed, hurt, and broken. I still had to make a conscious decision to walk in love, peace, joy, and not contention, outbursts of wrath, anger, or hatred.

I'm going to tell you this story. Some years back, I felt I was in a prison and not a home. My husband would come home from work with all these keys hanging off his waist. As he walked upstairs, I heard the keys jingling. I heard them as he came downstairs. As he got close to the last step, in my flesh I yelled, "Here comes the damn warden!"

Sad to say, the arguing started all over again. If and only if I would have said something in love, my night could've been peaceful. Look, I remember a singer by the name of Luther Vandross. He wrote a song, and the words went, "A chair is still a chair even when there's no one sitting there, but our chair is not a house, and a house is not a home when there's no one there to love you right." I made up that part.

However, if love is not present, a house will not be a home. Love will erase a lot of wrong, no matter what. The Bible says, above all, keep fervent in your love for one another because love covers a multitude of sins. Proverbs 10:12 (NIV) says, "Hatred stirs up conflict, but love covers over all wrong." Walking in the spirit of love will stop a lot of unnecessary shenanigans. Love has caused a change inside of me. I find it to be a little easier to walk according to the spirit of love than the lust of my flesh.

I feel him now as I'm writing. Praise your name, Jesus. Speak to me Lord. Forget about your husband, and tell God about yourself and how you need help in different areas of your life. While the Lord is working on you first and help getting you through those roughest times, be thankful for the entire things you have been through and still have my right mind.

Thank you, Jesus. Somebody didn't come through. They lost his or her mind, in a psych ward or jail for killing his or her mate. Lord, I thank you for keeping your hands on me. Oh, the Lord is good. As a prophetess of the Lord, I prophesy on this day of December 27, 2003, your house will turn into a home, you and your husband will be on one accord, he will love you as Christ loves the church, and you will submit as unto the Lord. Both of you will start to submit one to another, answer in a kind way, stop being hateful toward one another, and bear with one another during bad days as well as our good days. It is done in Jesus's name.

Satan, I serve you notice today. I decree and declare in every house you lose you hold on God's people. Marriages will be restored and made new, and they will begin loving each other. He will no longer see her as his enemy, and she will no longer say, "I hate that I married him." In the name of Jesus, it is finished, devil. In 2004, marriages will come together full force.

S-U-B-M-I-T

Surrendering, Under, Basic, Methods, Illustration, and Teaching

As God-elect lady, I try to do much as the Word states concerning a wife. I made some bad decisions and dumb choices, but it did not take away God's call on my life. Inasmuch, I chose to surrender to the Lord, and he taught me how to submit. I didn't want to submit because it felt as if I were weak. I always heard, "A woman is to submit to her husband," meaning she is to do what he says. I thought to myself, *The devil is a lie.*

As I search the word "submit," Webster's definition said to yield to the control or power of another, to give in to, and to yield to. Although God wants us to yield (surrender), I still felt some type of way about it, just to think he is telling me what to do. If I want God's blessing, all his commandments are planned for my good. Now I must freely drop the world's way of thinking, get understanding, and obey his will. The Bible is my manual for daily living. There are instructions on how to put things together when everything is out of place. I had to read the instructions from the beginning. We just started doing things and not reading the instructions, the Word of God, which caused a big headache.

So God, being El-Dibbor (almighty), merciful, and all loving in spite of my mess-ups, comes and put things back together again. He directs me through the Word and begins to demonstrate the basic methods, illustrations, and teachings on how to submit and start all over again. I found footnotes in Ephesians 5, and it states, "Submitting is taking the divinely order place in a relationship. Submitting can never be required by one human being of another. It can only be given on the basis of trust, that is, to believe God's Word and to be willing to learn to grow in a relationship."

How powerful is that. Submitting to the Word of God will cause growth! Wow! I wanted to grow. Proverb 14:1 says, "The wise woman builds her house, but the foolish pulls it down with her hands." I decided to become a wise woman and not a foolish one. I'd help build, putting things together instead of pulling down, straining, and messing up things.

For example, I wanted to be in my flesh. I cooked some hot dogs for my daughter, and I asked her how many she wanted. The Holy Spirit said, "Ask him how many he wants."

In my flesh, I didn't want to. I felt he was mean and hateful. I was not fixing him anything. My spirit submitted to the voice of the Holy Spirit. In obedience, his kind answer, yes, helped me spiritually. As long as he was rude, I should demonstrate kindness. I did not grow in this area expeditiously. It took a few years for me to grasp submitting. Fighting, yelling, and cursing appear as a foolish woman tearing down her own house with her hands. Hurt, pain, and betrayal evoked me to behave as a foolish woman sabotaging everything in my view, believing this would wound him equivalent to the hurt I felt. Wrong!

Howbeit, I am married to a person who believes "you cannot tell me anything." He knows it all and is full of pride. Baby, that meant I had to stay down on my knees a lot more. Honey, I had to pull out my weapons, but not guns or knives. It was the whole armor of God, which I mentioned earlier pertaining to the helmet of salvation.

"Finally, my brethren, be strong in the Lord and in the power of His might. Put on the whole armor of God that you may be able to stand against the wiles of the devil. For we do not wrestle against flesh and blood, but against principalities, against powers, against the rulers of the darkness of this age, against spiritual hosts of wickedness in heavenly places" (Eph. 6:10–12 Spirit-Filled Bible).

Armor: any defensive or protective covering for body in battle
Whole: complete; entire
Stand: to place upright; to endure; to undergo; to sustain
Wiles: plans; schemes used to deceive, entrap, and enslave you (Webster)

As a matter of fact, the revelation I received deriving out of this verse put on the entire, complete defensive covering, so you may be able to remain at rest in an upright position so you can see the plans. He will use his schemes to deceive, entrap, and enslave you. The enemy within me tried to enslave me with hurt, rejection, unforgiveness, and pain due to the adultery that took place in my marriage.

Yes, he watered another lawn, and he noticed I wasn't accepting that kind of behavior in my marriage. I endured it for some years for the reason he would say, "Please, I'm not going to do it again," but he'd manage to continue to do it over and over again. The Bible said, if you know your mate has committed adultery, you are free. I'm paraphrasing in my words.

I knew in my heart he was, but I didn't catch him in the act I always heard prove it. Listen. When I tell you a woman intuition is strong, it's strong. I always felt he was being unfaithful. I just didn't have the proof anyway. One morning he was in such a hurry to leave for work that he forgot his lunch. I asked myself, "Why is he in such a hurry?"

The very next day, he was in a hurry so I waited till he left. I jumped in my car and followed him. He did not notice I was on the next street, driving side by side. However, I had to turn on the same street he was on I was approximately ten cars behind him until I got caught at red light when it turned green. I was driving like Speedy Gonzales. I thought I lost him until I came up to this street and saw his car. I lost the sense of caring about nothing but hurting this man. I got out of my car, the Lexus he bought, and looked in his car. And when he saw my face, his eyes were as big as watermelons. He wouldn't unlock his door, but he tried to drive off I jumped in my car and I ran the Lexus into his car, where he couldn't move. They were stuck together.

I tore up his car and the Lexus. I had to move the Lexus so he could drive off. After that, he was so scared of what I might do to him. He took off again. I didn't chase him, but I went back home and cried for a long time. My heart was broken. I started my plans to leave. It took about three months. He did not know I was leaving. He thought everything was good.

After a while, I continued to do what I did before this happened until the day of my departure. I gathered up enough money for an apartment and items for it, and I left. He came home to find his wife and child was gone. I didn't tell him anything. He did not know where I lived, nor the school our daughter attended.

After a few months, I called to check on him. Of course there was the crying, "I'm sorry," and "I want do it again. I changed." As a woman of the faith, I said okay and believed what he said, but I had some doubts he was just telling me what I wanted to hear.

By the grace of God, I didn't pull out my flesh weapon that could've caused him some intense pain. I used some of the other ones though—cussing, calling him names, breaking things, and not cooking for him. The prophetess went out in the deep for a season and used all of what he did to justify why I behaved like a foolish woman. I wanted him to feel guilt, stress, shame, and the embarrassment as I felt.

No one knew of this, apart from him and myself. Shame and embarrassment shut my mouth on account of him being a minister at that time. I just couldn't believe he would've done this as a man of God, but I realized they were human and not exempt from being enticed, tempted, and lured if they were not suited up with the armor of God.

Nevertheless, time went on, and my whole attitude transformed from one degree to another. I started to focus on what he was doing, saying, and going instead of praying and asking God for help. I was consumed with if he were still cheating. I thought I could do it by myself without the counseling of God. To make God laugh, tell him your plans. As an illustration, my husband decided to clean up the back patio. We had a few flowers planted back there, all of which died except one standing by itself.

As I looked out the window to see what he was doing, I noticed the flower, and the Lord spoke to my heart, "All the flowers died except that one."

I asked him, "What does that mean?"

He replied, "He raked all around the flower bed and pulled up the dead flowers. That one still standing is you. Though you stand lonely and alone, you are not alone. You made it through the valley of the shadow of death. I said I would never leave you nor forsake you."

Thereafter, I wrote a letter to my husband, stating what God imparted in my heart and by whose help I felt the need we together would seek counseling.

With no attempt, he said, "I don't need counseling."

Because of his statement, I was under the impression he didn't consider our marriage to be salvageable. That is, during this point, his mind was consumed with lies the devil injected through his thoughts. Unfortunately he failed to put on his headgear, the helmet of salvation, and resist the enemy.

The Breast Plate of Righteousness

Shield of Faith
Girded your waist with truth
Shod Your Feet with the Preparation of Peace
Sword of the Spirit, which is the Word of God
The Helmet of Salvation

If you notice, the armor of God is made to protect every vital part of the body. Check it out! The helmet of salvation is designed to protect your mind. The Bible says, "Do not conform to the pattern of this world, but be transformed by the renewing of you mind" (Rom. 12:2). There's an illustration a few pages back of the mind and the components—thoughts, logic, intellect, imagination, and reasoning—which sums up understanding and changing the way we think. Second Corinthians 5:17 (KJV) says, "Therefore, if anyone is in Christ, he is a new creation; old things pass away behold all things become new."

Changing our thoughts is a process for the following:

1. We don't like to be uncomfortable. We rather stay how we are much easier.
2. No one wants to humble himself or herself. Thoughts of you want to make no fool out of me.
3. There is a lack of discipline. Not spending the quality time in the Word of God as we should can cause negative thoughts. We ask the question why, as Christians, we still struggle in our thoughts with temptations, bitterness, depression, fear, doubts, and frustration. And the list goes on.
4. We think with our mind, desire with our will, and feel with our emotions. God will not renew your mind. The Word says, "Renew your mind." You renew your own mind by reading what God has promised us in his Word. Changing the way we think is our responsibility. God is there to help us through this process, but we first must obey his Word. Get in there and protect your mind from the deceitful lies the devil injects in your thoughts and imagination. Put on the helmet!

The Breastplate of Righteousness

Be right in all you are doing! An armed soldier wears a breastplate made of metal, prepared for battle in the natural. It is worn to protect the vital parts, namely the heart and soul, from the adversary's deception. The belt of truth is worn tightly. It goes right along with the breastplate righteousness. By wearing the breastplate of righteousness, we begin to generate a clean heart that will transform into transaction.

For example, I went to Arkansas to visit my mother for a few weeks, and my husband kept calling all day and all night. I went to get some peace, restoration, and healing. As the calls continued to come, my emotions were off the chart. My flesh was ready to speak just how I was really feeling.

I never forget this. It was around 9:00 a.m. their time, and my phone was ringing and ringing and ringing. I had ignored some of his calls. I looked to see who was calling, and it was my husband. All of a sudden, I felt anger like no other. I said, "I am going to tell his butt off! I'll tell him that he hurt and embarrassed me and how he treated me like a doormat."

I picked up the phone. "Hello!"

He said, "Pat, please forgive me." He was sobbing like a baby. I sensed the sincerity in his voice.

Right at that moment, the Holy Spirit spoke to me, "If that were you, how would you want to be restored?"

Instantly my heart felt his hurt, and at that moment, I forgot all the bad deeds he had committed toward me. My breastplate of righteousness and belt of truth were in effect. Instantly I began to minister to the man of God. My hurt and pain went away. From that day, I made sure my heart did what was right regardless how I was treated. The power of God inside me equipped me to do that.

The Shield of Faith

I have read somewhere that the Roman shield was huge, the size of a door, and would protect them fully. The shield is used as a defensive weapon and to push back the adversary. Clearly the shield is used as a protection in all situations. It keeps the darts of the devil away from hitting the head and heart. The attacks from the devil sometimes cause me to lose hope in God, especially when the belligerence comes from the closest person next to me. Nevertheless, without faith, it is impossible to please God.

For instance, I was brought up old school. My parents were from the country. When you buy salt pork, you put it in the cabinet for weeks or even months because it makes the pork taste old. I didn't know my husband would see the meat in the cabinet and think I was doing witchcraft. The fiery darts he would speak toward me would pierce my heart.

Well, we had an argument, and he said, "You are a witch. You are not a prophetess. You are a psychic. Where's your crystal ball?"

He wouldn't go by that cabinet, thinking a spell would get on him. He called his mother and told her, if anything happened to him, I was using witchcraft on him.

She responded, "What are you talking about?"

He began telling her about the meat in the cabinet. It's funny now, but it wasn't then. He asked her, "Did you know anything about that?"

She said, "Yea! Boy, you are crazy. That girl ain't putting no witchcraft on you. She letting the meat get old, so when she cooking greens, it makes them taste better."

I put up my shield of faith to block what the enemy meant for evil. Faith is not what I see but what I cannot see. It is simply given to me by God. He said in Matthew 17:20, "Jesus said unto them because of your unbelief: for verily I say unto you, if ye have faith as a grain of mustard seed." So the conclusion is, as tiny as the mustard seed is, I should have faith even if it is tiny faith. By continuing to have faith, it will grow to big faith. In addition, the book of Hebrews will build up your faith. I call it the faith manual.

The armor of God is designed to perfectly fit each person who has enlisted in the army of God. I can't put on my husband's armor because it's made only for him. I have to put on the armor that was designed for me. I need to know every piece, what it is for, and how I need to use the defensive or offensive weapon. I can't use my helmet when it is time to use my shield of faith. I can't use my breastplate of righteousness when it's time to shod my feet with the preparation of the gospel of peace. Can you hear what I'm saying? By putting on the complete armor of God, I can look the devil in his face and say, "You can't touch this!"

You and I are in the army. We are in a spiritual warfare. It is time for us to use our spiritual weapon that God has made for you and me. Make sure we aim at the right target and use the correct pieces for that particular circumstance because we do not want friendly fire, meaning to cause injury or casualties toward one another. We need to pray and ask God to show us how to use the weapons so they can be effective when we start to shoot our artillery. This is the most important thing we need before putting on the whole armor of God because we are in a spiritual warfare and fighting things unseen in the air, demonic forces that our worst adversary, the devil himself, has sent.

First Peter 5:8–9 (Spirit-Filled Bible) tells us, "Be sober; be vigilant, because your adversary the devil walks about like a roaring lion, seeking whom he may devour resist him, steadfast in the faith. Knowing that the same sufferings are experienced by your brotherhood in the world."

As a pastor's and a minister's wife, I was afraid to tell the truth about struggles I faced in my marriage, which was okay during that season. As a result of my struggles, hard times, brokenness, and hurts, the Lord allowed me to go through it just to be able to tell my testimony. During that particular period of time, I asked, "Why am I being treated this way?"

The Lord said in a small voice, "What you are going through is not for you but for someone else!"

All the tests I failed over, over, over, and over again, I didn't know it would be my story. Not to mention a pastor's or minister's wife is a hard job. All the masks I had to wear—happy mask, "I'm blessed" mask, and "You are my cream in my coffee" mask—just covered up pain and hurt! I call it the concealer of pretend. The concealer covers up blemishes, and it comes in different types of coverage.

To put it another way, I was so broken that I cried and prayed every day about my situation. One Sunday morning while getting ready for service, I looked in the mirror to make sure my concealer for hurt was on evenly because, when I got to church, I didn't want to look as if I had put on the concealer. Every time I left home, I put on concealer to cover up all the various blemishes that might show on my face.

Nevertheless, I perceive, if you have no understanding concerning hard times and struggles in marriages or anything else for that matter, how can you help a person who is going through various trials? I understand the spirit can guide you through the Word and encourage them. For example, one marriage class I attended was to help build your marriage. The husband and wife teaching portrayed this picture- perfect marriage. First, there's no such thing as a perfect marriage. They were somewhat aware of my circumstance. As I sat there and listened to this stuff, it didn't sit well in my spirit. I don't believe God intend for men or woman in the gospel to point out to be jealous and insecure in the ministry.

Although they impersonated their marriage to be rock-solid, I discerned deception, sadness, trouble, and disconnect. After the class was over, I got in my car and began to pray, "Lord, if you ever place me in a position to help your people, I wouldn't make them feel less than I feel now." Sad to say, that marriage ended up splitting apart.

Tell the bad half testimony. Tell how hard it was to stay in the marriage, how an adulteress spirit evaded your marriage, and how miserable it was to have intimacy with him after the infidelity. Keep it real but holy! Revelation 12:11 say, "And they overcame him by the blood of the lamb, and by the word of their testimony not testifony!"

Being sensitive to the spirit, he leads me to say what I thought I wouldn't ever tell, my true testimony:

1. When my husband didn't come home
2. Phone numbers he should not have
3. Sleeping on the couch and not in the bed

The very things I tried to keep quit, God said to release it. Someone was facing various trials. God said, "Let my daughter know that I have not forgotten her. I see what's taking place. Do not worry about your husband. I want you. Allow me to put you on the potter's wheel and mold and shape you into a beautiful teacup I designed for you."

Woman of God, God has not forgotten you! He said he would never leave you nor forsake you. Hold your head up and stand firm in what God has told you. Yet in all these things, we are more than conquerors through him who loved us (Rom. 8:37 AB). God's Word is a promise, and what he said in it, He will perform it. His word will not return unto him void, but accomplish what it was sent to do.

In addition, in order to get the promises of God, there will be conditions. Make sure we meet them. When the Lord says what he is going to do, we must keep our part. For instance, "if my people who are called by my name will humble themselves, and pray and seek my face and turn from their wicked ways, then I will hear from heaven, and will forgive their sin and heal their land" (2 Chronicles. 7:14 NIV). The word "if" is a choice. He has given us a free will to choose to obey by humbling ourselves, seeking his face, praying, and turning from our wicked ways. For obedience is the promise he will hear from heaven, forgive our sin, and heal our land.

Keep in mind. For every promise, there is a condition. I read his promises and thought they were there for me to have. I did not know that I had requirements to do in order for him to perform. I had no knowledge until I started going to Bible studies, prayed, fasted, and stayed around spirit-filled people. I wanted to know more about the Lord, and staying around the anointing has given me clarification about his promise.

Father, in the name of Jesus, I pray today that I will submit to my own husband as unto the Lord. In spite of want, I hear and see. Help me to stay humble and always first to say sorry to my husband. In the name of Jesus, help every woman who is reading this book. You have inspired me to write. Help me to submit. Not every woman has that problem, Lord, but help us who do have the problem. I give you thanks and praise for it right now in the mighty and powerful name of Jesus. I am standing on the Word of God, knowing it is working for our good.

I hear the Holy Spirit talking to me as I am writing. There is a woman who feels like she is at her rope's end. Your husband is thinking about walking out on you, and you have no reason why. The Lord said it is all right. He's there with you at this moment. Do not lose the faith. Continuing to stand on his Word, your faith is what made your husband surrender the first time.

Now it will be your faith that will keep him there. My daughter, I am taking you to the next level of faith. It might seem to be hard, but there is nothing too hard for me, says the Lord. Thank you, Jesus, for your word of faith. I hear the name K. J.

So remember—we must every day put on the armor that God he has molded for you and me for daily combat. It will never fail us. In conclusion, the armor of God will make us strong and mighty and strengthen us where we are weak. God's Word will give us unspeakable joy, peace, self-control, and love. Today has been an awesome day.

Respecting One Another

Today, o Lord, I give praise and honor for giving me the ability to continue this assignment you placed in my heart. Lord, use me for your glory in Jesus's name. You know, I was lying in my bed, and I heard the word "respect." I said "respect." I went and looked up the definition to see what it meant. (Webster's says respect is to fall or show honor or esteem for; to show consideration; to honor high regard, glory, and regard to look at attentively; to concern or involve; relation in regard to your plan).

Well, all men want respect, but their definition is a little off from Webster's. I notice that sometimes when they say respect me they are saying, "Listen to me and do what I tell you to do." Not that women intentionally disregard what our husbands ask of us. The reason would be due to bad behavior and disrespecting. Period! This makes it a little difficult to give the honor they insist their wife should give. Romans 12:10 (Spirit-Filled Bible) says, "Be kindly affectionate to one another with brotherly love, in honor giving preference to one another." Also Philippians 2:3 say, "Let nothing be done through selfish ambition or conceit, but in lowliness of mind let each esteem others better then himself."

As I think about respect, consideration is respect. I consider my husband before I make any decision that might cause conflict. I honor him with my body and love him with my action versus how he defines respect.

He says, "I go to work, provide, and pay all the bills. I'm head of the house, and you should submit to authority." So he says.

With that attitude, I bucked like a horse, meaning I was defiant. I rebelled and had a smart mouth. In light of I not respecting him with my words at home, I did outside of the home. With that in mind, whenever I was apart from him, I never talked about him to others in a disrespectful way or converse with another man concerning my bad marriage. Men want to be treated like kings. They want to hear how wonderful they are, along with how appreciated they are, how good they smell, and how no one else could love him the you way love him. And so on so on so on and so on. I want to hear those exact words from my husband as well.

My husband had experienced several bad relationships, which caused a scar deep in his heart. I never understood why he would be so mean, sharp with his words, and disengaged. That deep scar in his heart caused him to put up a wall of defense to block love from coming in and going out. Every time I would show love toward him, he would reject it. His action showed he didn't care. As a matter of fact, he would say, "I don't care. I'm not in love with you."

That wounded me to the core of me soul. I prayed and asked God, "Why?"

For a while, I didn't receive an answer from the Lord until one day he came home from work and I asked how his day was. He looked at me with hate in his eyes and said, "Can you wait till I get in the door good enough before you start asking me questions?"

At that moment, the Lord told me why he was that way. I said to him, "Don't make me pay for what your ex did to you! I'm not her, and you are treating me based on what she did to hurt you. Stop making me suffer for something I did not do!"

Although this might be true, he continued to stuff his emotion and kept me at a long distance for a while. As time passed, he opened up and began to tell me all the things that happened that caused his heart to be hard. He went on to say, "I never let anyone in my heart again."

However, when you block love, you will not be able to receive love nor show love in a way God has purposed for him to love. Ephesians 5:2 (NKJV) says, "Walk in the way of love just as Christ also has loved us and given himself for us." I am still talking about respect. Everyone wants to be respected, especially in a marriage. Although it has been shown little in my marriage, I still believe God can and will show me mercy and work it out for my good. The enemy has been trying to destroy my marriage since 1999 because he knew we would be a power team when we became one. Let's go on a little further with respect.

The first thing to remember is that respect is essential in a marriage. Without it, there is no marriage. Let me fence myself. I am not judging no one marriage nor coming up against no one marriage. By the same token, God designed marriages to be a holy union between a husband and wife (Gen. 2:23 KJV). Anything outside of that, please feel free to take it upon yourself to go to the one who designed it that way.

Now back to what I was saying. Respect is thoughtful, courteous, and kind. Respect means treating each other with deep admiration. Respect is not dominant, authoritative, or commanding. I recall watching a program on TV about prison life, and I heard one of the men say he demanded respect. And if they did not get it, they took action, and the action toward the other person was aggressive and deadly just for respect.

What does this have to do with marriages, prophetess? Provided that a woman has lost her life because her husband felt she wasn't respecting him the way he felt she should, that kind of respect is definitely not how God planned or designed for a husband or wife. Love and respect works hand in hand when my husband respects me, putting me before all others and himself. Automatically, I naturally love him although he has treated me like dirt. I pray you understand what I am trying to articulate to you concerning respect.

The day my husband stopped respecting me was the day he didn't respect himself, being that we are no longer two individuals but one, according to Matthew 19:6 (NIV), "so they are no longer two, but one flesh."

First, when my husband committed adultery, he broke the covenant he made between God and himself, which caused division. The respect to honor and esteem was no longer there for him when the adultery took place. It definitely brought in separation, and then division took over in our marriage. What he does with his body affects what I do with mine. It affects him because we are joined together as one. "Therefore a man shall leave his father and mother and hold fast to his wife and they shall be one flesh. (Gen. 2:24 NIV). "He who loves his wife loves himself" (Eph. 5:28 NIV).

Esteem means to value highly. When my husband started to value what the Lord had given him, I automatically began to respect him. I had no problem of doing what he asked me to do. When he put me above himself according to Philippians 2:3, how beautiful it would be putting me before anything or anyone—before the kids, his job, parents, siblings, and pastor. The only one who comes before me is the Lord God Almighty himself. I wouldn't mind at all taking second place to the Lord. I believe, if he is in love with the Lord, he automatically will know how to love and respect me. As a sidebar, don't pray and ask the Lord for a husband. Ask for a man who is so in love with God that he will already know how to love and respect you.

By Loving You, I Love Myself

First Peter 3:7 says, "Husbands, likewise, dwell with them with understanding, giving honor to the wife, as to the weaker vessel, and as being heirs together of the grace of life, that your prayers may not be hindered."

My husband is to consider me being the lesser one in physical strength and vulnerability. He has to realize, as my husband, he has a responsibility of treating me kind, showing honor, listening to me, spending time with me, and making me feel extremely important. By not doing so, his prayers will be hindered. God will not hear them at all. Why? Because he has not honored the gift God has blessed him with.

Genesis 2:18–19 says,

> And the Lord God said, "It is not good that man should be alone: I will make him a helper comparable to him." Out of the ground the Lord God formed every beast; He even made man from the ground verse ... The Lord God cause Adam to fall in a deep sleep and took one of his ribs, and closed up the flesh in its place. Then the rib, which the Lord God has taken from man, He made into a woman, and He brought her to the man.

The Lord just presented him a gift! Anytime someone brings a present or gives you something, it is a gift. It is your responsibility to take of the gift that was given to you. Or you will just throw it aside and say, "I don't want this" or "I don't like this." You just showed disrespect for what was given to you.

He who finds a wife finds a good thing and obtains favor from the Lord. Adam was excited about his wife. He loved his wife, he spent time with her, he cherished her, and he did all the things God had spoken to him to do. I like where it said God brought her to him. Adam did not have to go and look for his wife. God brought her to Adam and presented his wife to him.

Therefore, by reading these scriptures, God did not want man to go look for or find a wife. God gave Adam his wife after he worked and took care of the garden. In addition, after he finished his work, God saw it was not good for man to be alone and gave him his wife.

Father, in the name of Jesus, I hope this book will help those who have been struggling, and I thank you. I pray for women who sometimes feel lonely in their marriage, but knowing we are not alone. Help me today, Lord, to continue to write what you are speaking into my spirit to say.

And Lord, I pray that people will recognize and take this book as an encouragement and tool help. Pastor's and Minister's wives encounter many things that are difficult and hurtful. Not only the women in ministry, but the ones outside the ministry as well. Father, I give thanks and praise for what you have done and what you are going to do. In Jesus's name, I pray.

When God has gracefully gifted us with something, we should cherish, honor, and respect it. During a time of struggles and trials in my life, I was a single mother without a car, riding buses and hitching rides to get from one place to another. I never called my dad and asked him for anything. I tried to do it on my own without asking for help. Walking back and forth in the rain to get my daughter to school was terrible. I decided to call my dad and ask if he had an extra car I could have to take my baby to school and complete other things I needed to do.

He said, "Yes, come out to the yard, and get this truck. It's not a new truck. It has some damage to it, but it has AC."

I was excited. I hitched a ride to my dad's company, and when I arrived, he had the truck in front of the office. Ya'll when I tell you it was ugly, it was ugly! The color was gray. The back of the truck was damaged and looked as if it had been pushed up on the left side, but I was still excited because he gave me a gift. When I started it up, it sounded like ten motorbikes. I turned on the air-conditioning. It was so cold that I had to turn it off. Bakersfield is hot in the summers, 102 degrees or hotter, so I was happy. I could ride without cooking in the sun.

The moral to this story was that my dad gave me a gift. Although it was damaged and ugly, I took care of it as if were a brand-new vehicle. I washed, serviced, and vacuumed it. And I drove it with pride even though people laughed at it.

My husband was ugly in action and words, and he laughed at me. I struggled with respecting him because he didn't respect me, but God gave him to me. God said everything he made was good. Nevertheless, when two people are coming together as one or being joined together, it isn't an easy task. You see each other's mistakes and ugliest. You know when something is wrong with one another. We know when the day was a bad or good one. Let everyone of you in particular so love his own wife as himself, and let the wife see that she respects her husband (Eph. 5:33 KJV).

I have seen woman in the ministry show more respect for the pastors than their own husbands, which is wrong, no matter how the husband's conduct is. This causes the husband to have ill feeling toward the pastor. In his mind, he's thinking, "Who is he? He ain't God." How can you respect the pastor and submit to him as unto the Lord and not your own husband? That is not pleasing to God. His ministry starts in the home. Rather, the husband has a relationship with the Lord or not. You still respect him. He is your husband.

First Corinthians 7:14 (KJV) says, "For the unbelieving husband is sanctified by the wife, and the unbelieving wife, is sanctified by the husband; else were your children unclean; but now are they holy."

Showing holiness in your home around your husband activates the Word of God, and you can win over your unbelieving husband. (Holiness means to set apart and to be different from the world.) He sees your lifestyle, and now he is ready to receive Christ in his life. That is how we sanctify our husband. Letting him see God in you will change him, but if he sees you home from church, you are fussing, being a busybody, and gossiping. He might say nothing, but believe me, he is looking and listening to every word you say and every deed you do. Bishop G always says, "Either you will draw them or drive them." I made my mind up to be a drawer, letting my husband see Jesus in me.

By doing so, he can become a powerful and awesome man of God. Together walking in agreement, we can help marriages and bring restoration, being renewed to health, kids obeying the parents, and everything in its proper order. My prayer for everyone who is reading this book is that his or her marriage may prosper and be in good health. I love to see healthy relationships. It tells me that you fought for your marriage and you didn't give up. Although you had your share of ups, downs, bumps, bruises, and scars, you vowed to stay till death do you part. Stay on death row, and in the end, you will win!

After a period of time, the honeymoon phase is over. There comes a point when suddenly the unthinkable happens. You get frustrated with one another. I felt as if I were sharing the house with the character in *Nightmare on Elm Street*. You know who that is. Some nights I couldn't sleep. My kid was on my nerves. I wanted to quit my job. Bills were due. I thought about homicide and suicide, but Jesus would deliver. He came through for me during times of troubles and distress.

When I thought about walking away and leaving, Jesus sent a woman to speak a word of encouragement. She told me to stand and know that he would never leave me nor turn his back on me. The Word of God is alive. It is everything you and I need to make it through this cruel and awful world. The enemy designed daily issues you and I face in this world to destroy us spiritually, emotionally, physically, and economically. God's Word is the manual to win every fight, war, and battle. Reading the Word will bring hope, strength, the character of God, love, peace, joy, and long-suffering.

Father, thank you for your Son, Jesus. Lord, I thank you for your love, mercy, and kindness you have shown toward me. Father, in the name of Jesus, I am expecting you to pour out your love and bring peace in every home today in the mighty name of Jesus.

Love: to please; affection based on admiration
"Love is patient, love is kind. It does not envy, it does not boast, it is not proud" (1 Cor. 13:4 NIV).

Father, I am here today to say what you shared in my spirit. Father, I thank you for your Word and the Holy Spirit. Please help us heal from hurt, pain of love from our past, and rejection. Make us whole and complete in you. Restore our faith in love. Bring true love to us. We had trouble with love in times past that caused disappointments. Father, we choose to be healed right now. We choose to love and make new choices to reclaim the innocence of our heart in Jesus's name.

Love is a powerful tool. First Corinthians 13:4 (NIV) say, "Love is kind. It does not envy, it does not boast, it is not proud. It does not dishonor others, it is not self-seeking, it is not easily angered, it keeps no record of wrongs." I must say it was tough for me to show any type of love toward my husband over a period of years. He rejected me, abandoned me (stopped communication), separated himself (slept in different beds), and did not love me (put up a wall to protect his heart). I didn't want to feel like or be a fool for loving someone who didn't love me back. A song came to my mind, "It feels so good loving somebody and somebody loves you back." We know who sings this song. I haven't been saved all my life. I "tuned up," as the young folks would say, until I accepted the Lord. Then he turned me down. Come on, somebody. Can I get an Amen, or am I the only one who tuned up?

As I share my story, I want you to know all of the hurtful things I encountered in my marriage. God didn't plan it to destroy me, but it was to bring me to a place of maturity in him so I could help my husband spiritually, emotionally, and mentally. My adversary wished he could have destroyed both of us during the most devastating time of our marriage. The fasting and praying I did, God blocked what the enemy meant for evil and worked it for my good. Love is a beautiful thing. Who in their right mind would reject love? Only a fool!

"With thy love and kindness have I drawn thee" (Jer. 31:3 KJV).

How can I love my husband when he has mistreated and mentally abused me? How can I love him when he took me for granted? How can I love him when he says I'm his enemy? How can I love him? Should I treat him the way he treated me? Can I say things to destroy his self-esteem? These were the types of questions I asked God because I couldn't wrap around my head how my husband could say he loved the Lord but not loved the one God gave to him. As much as I wanted to open up my heart and love him with agape love, the pain, hurt, and mistrust blocked it. Whenever I would be in the same room with him, my feelings were out of control because of the way I was thinking toward him. The more I thought about everything he had done, the angrier I became.

I said, "Lord, help me to love this man the way you love him because in my own strength I cannot."

As I began to cry out, the Lord began to share these words with me, "Through all your mistakes and imperfections, I loved and forgave you. I have seen everything that happened, and I heard your cry. I will never leave you. I will always be there for you."

Tears began to soak my pillow. My hands lifted up, asking the Lord to forgive me. I didn't want to be angry and bitter but better. In order for me to get better, I had to forgive my husband. Furthermore, to forgive, I had to let go of the pain, hurt, anger, and bitterness, which wasn't easy to do because I kept feeling like I was right based on my pain. After I made a choice to release everything that happened, first I embraced the pain. I felt the pain. Then I let it go. I found it to be much easier letting things go rather than holding on to it and being bound to that condition emotionally, which was strong as stone.

"Love keeps no record" (1 Cor. 13:5 NIV).

Love holds no accounts of shortcoming/wrongs that have been done to one other. We should not walk around each other with bad attitudes but rather with positive ones. God does not keep a list of the mistakes, wrongs, and sins we have done. He says, "He will again have compassion on us, He will tread our sins underfoot and hurl all our iniquities into the depths of the sea to remember them no more" (Micah 7:19 KJV).

The Lord has compassion for me and is full of tender mercies and never failing. He forgives all my sins and never held it against me in his heart, and he doesn't remember any more toward me. As far as the east is from the west, so far has he removed my transgressions from me. That's love. While I'm writing, I'm thinking about how he never brought up the times I cussed out my husband, tore up his clothes, wrecked the car, whooped on him, and stopped cooking for him. He's not holding it against me.

I wasn't supposed to keep record of it, nor harbor it or dwell on the mistreatments I received from my spouse. God didn't do it to me. Love lets things go, such as anger, hurt, bitterness, and resentment, so I won't destroy my marriage. Love is a fruit, but fruit of the spirit is love, joy peace, long-suffering, kindness, goodness, faithfulness, gentleness, and self-control against such there is no law (Gal. 5:22 NIV). I struggled with producing the fruit of love, and in order for me to walk in love I had to birth love.

What do you mean, "birth love"? For example, when a woman starts to labor before delivering her baby, she experiences a great amount of pain. In Genesis 3:16, God said to the woman, "I will make your pains in childbearing very severe with painful labor you will give birth to children."

We all know why he said it. If you don't know why, read all of Genesis 3. It will explain why God said it to Eve. During the pain, she might say, "I can't take this pain. Please give me something to take away this pain." And right before pushing out her baby, she say "I cannot. I can't do it." All of a sudden, the head is out, the baby is out, and instantly she feels the joy to see her baby and the unconditional love felt for her baby. In same manner, during the period of bearing love for my husband was with great pain, I cried out for help. I said, "I can't do this. I quit. I'm done." As I continued to push through the pain, love came and freed me.

**"Whoever does not love does not know God,
because God is love" (1 John 4:8 NIV).**

Father, I thank you today for your Son. You made him who had no sin to be sin for us, so that in him we might become the righteousness of God. Lord, you so loved the world that you gave your one and only Son that whoever believes in him shall not perish but have eternal life. I thank you in advance for pouring out your love and mercy on others and me when we do not deserve it. By faith I will love unconditionally my husband and everyone I encounter, even if they do not deserve it in that name that is above all other names, Jesus.

In conclusion, my prayer for you is something I have shared with you. I bless you because I am tremendously honored that God has allowed me to write my story of a *Minister Wife: Married Lonely But Not Alone.* Although the pain I endured was worth it, I don't know if I would do it again. But praise God I made it through, and my husband and I are walking together in love after twenty-two years of marriage. The Lord Bless and keep you. May the Lord make his face shine on you and be gracious to you. And may the Lord turn his face toward you and give you peace. I love you!

Made in the USA
Las Vegas, NV
04 December 2020

12005561R00042